Lysistrata

ARISTOPHANES

LYSISTRATA

TRANSLATED BY ALAN H. SOMMERSTEIN

PENGUIN BOOKS

PENGUIN BOOKS

Published by the Penguin Group

Penguin Books USA Inc., 375 Hudson Street,
New York, New York 10014, U.S.A.
Penguin Books Ltd, 27 Wrights Lane,
London W8 5TZ, England
Penguin Books Australia Ltd, Ringwood,
Victoria, Australia
Penguin Books Canada Ltd, 10 Alcorn Avenue,
Toronto, Ontario, Canada M4V 3B2
Penguin Books (N.Z.) Ltd, 182–190 Wairau Road,
Auckland 10, New Zealand

Penguin Books Ltd, Registered Offices:
Harmondsworth, Middlesex, England

Published in Penguin Books 1995

This play is from *Lysistrata and Other Plays* by Aristophanes,
translated by Alan H. Sommerstein, published by Penguin Books.

ISBN 0 14 60.0166 4

Printed in the United States of America

Characters

LYSISTRATA
CALONICE } *Athenian women*
MYRRHINE
LAMPITO *a Spartan woman*
CHORUS OF OLD MEN
CHORUS OF OLD WOMEN
STRATYLLIS *leader of the Women's Chorus*
A MAGISTRATE *member of the Committee of Ten*
    for the Safety of the State
FIVE YOUNG WOMEN
CINESIAS *husband to Myrrhine*
BABY *son to Cinesias and Myrrhine*
A SPARTAN HERALD
A SPARTAN AMBASSADOR
AN ATHENIAN NEGOTIATOR
TWO LAYABOUTS
DOORKEEPER *of the Acropolis*
TWO DINERS

ISMENIA *a Boeotian woman*
A CORINTHIAN WOMAN
RECONCILIATION *maidservant to Lysistrata*
FOUR SCYTHIAN POLICEMEN
A SCYTHIAN POLICEWOMAN
ATHENIAN CITIZENS, SPARTAN
   AMBASSADORS, ATHENIAN AND SPARTAN
   WOMEN, SLAVES, *etc.*

Act One

SCENE: *In front of the entrance to the Athenian Acropolis. At the back of the stage stands the Great Gateway (the Propylaea); to the right, a stretch of the Acropolis wall with a little shrine to Athena Niké (Victory) built into it; to the left, a statue of the tyrannicides Harmodius and Aristogeiton. It is early morning.*

[LYSISTRATA *is standing in front of the Propylaea looking, with increasing impatience, to see if anyone is coming.*]

LYSISTRATA [*stamping her foot and bursting into impatient speech*]: Just think if it had been a Bacchic celebration they'd been asked to attend – or something in honour of Pan or Aphrodite – particularly Aphrodite! You wouldn't have been able to move for all the drums. And now look – not a woman here!

   [*Enter* CALONICE.]

Ah! here's one at last. One of my neighbours, I – Why, hello, Calonice.

3

CALONICE: Hello, Lysistrata. What's bothering you, dear? Don't screw up your face like that. It really doesn't suit you, you know, knitting your eyebrows up like a bow or something.

LYSISTRATA: Sorry, Calonice, but I'm furious. I'm disappointed in womankind. All our husbands think we're such clever villains –

CALONICE: Well, aren't we?

LYSISTRATA: And here I've called a meeting to discuss a very important matter, and they're all still fast asleep!

CALONICE: Don't worry, dear, they'll come. It's not so easy for a wife to get out of the house, you know. They'll all be rushing to and fro for their husbands, waking up the servants, putting the baby to bed or washing and feeding it –

LYSISTRATA: Damn it, there are more important things than that!

CALONICE: Tell me, Lysistrata dear, what is it you've summoned this meeting of the women for? Is it something big?

LYSISTRATA: Very.

CALONICE [*thinking she detects a significant intonation in that word*]: Not thick as well?

4

LYSISTRATA: As a matter of fact, yes.

CALONICE: Then why on earth aren't they here?

LYSISTRATA [*realizing she has been misleading*]: No, not that kind of thing — well, not exactly. If it had been, I can assure you, they'd have been here as quick as you can bat an eyelid. No, I've had an idea, which for many sleepless nights I've been tossing to and fro —

CALONICE: Must be a pretty flimsy one, in that case.

LYSISTRATA: Flimsy? Calonice, we women have the salvation of Greece in our hands.

CALONICE: In our hands? We might as well give up hope, then.

LYSISTRATA: The whole future of the City is up to us. Either the Peloponnesians are all going to be wiped out —

CALONICE: Good idea, by Zeus!

LYSISTRATA: — and the Boeotians be destroyed too —

CALONICE: Not all of them, please! Do spare the eels.

LYSISTRATA: — and Athens — well, I won't say it, but you know what might happen. But if all the women join together — not just us, but the Peloponnesians and Boeotians as well — then we can save Greece.

CALONICE: The women! — what could they ever do

that was any use? Sitting at home putting flowers in their hair, putting on cosmetics and saffron gowns and Cimberian see-through shifts, with slippers on our feet?

LYSISTRATA: But don't you see, that's exactly what I mean to use to save Greece. Those saffron gowns and slippers and see-through dresses, yes, and our scent and rouge as well.

CALONICE: How are you going to do that?

LYSISTRATA: I am going to bring it about that the men will no longer lift up their spears against one another —

CALONICE: I'm going to get some new dye on my yellow gown!

LYSISTRATA: — nor take up their shields —

CALONICE: I'll put on a see-through right away!

LYSISTRATA: — or their swords.

CALONICE: Slippers, here I come!

LYSISTRATA: *Now* do you think the women ought to be here by now?

CALONICE: By Zeus, yes — they ought to have taken wing and flown here.

LYSISTRATA: No such luck, old girl; what do you expect? — they're Athenian, and everything they do too late. But really – for nobody to have come at all! None from the Paralia, none of the Salaminians –

CALONICE: Oh, they'll have been on the go since the small hours. [*Aside*] They probably will too.

LYSISTRATA: And the ones I was most counting on being here first – the Acharnians – they haven't come either.

CALONICE: Well, as to that, I did see Theagenes' wife consulting the shrine of Hecate in front of her door, so I imagine she's going to come.

[*Enter, from various directions,* MYRRHINE *and other women.*]

Ah, here are some coming – and here are some more. Ugh! [*puckering up her nose*] Where do this lot come from?

LYSISTRATA: Ponchidae.

CALONICE: I can well believe it!

MYRRHINE [*a little out of breath*]: We're not late, are we, Lysistrata?

[LYSISTRATA *frowns and says nothing.*]

Well? Why aren't you saying anything?

LYSISTRATA: Myrrhine, I don't think much of people who come this late when such an important matter is to be discussed.

MYRRHINE [*lamely*]: Well, I had some difficulty finding my girdle in the dark. If it is so important, don't let's wait for the rest; tell us about it now.

LYSISTRATA: Let's just wait a moment. The Boeotian and Peloponnesian women should be here any time now.

MYRRHINE: Good idea. Ah, here comes Lampito!

[*Enter* LAMPITO, *with several other Spartan women, their dresses fringed at the bottom with sheepskin, and with representatives from Corinth and Boeotia.*]

LYSISTRATA: Welcome, Lampito, my dear. How are things in Sparta? Darling, you look simply beautiful. Such colour, such resilience! Why, I bet you could throttle a bull.

LAMPITO: Sae cuid you, my dear, if ye were in training. Dinna ken, I practise rump-jumps every day.

LYSISTRATA [*prodding her*]: And such marvellous tits, too.

LAMPITO [*indignantly*]: I'd thank ye not tae treat me as though ye were just aboot tae sacrifice me.

LYSISTRATA: Where's this other girl come from?

LAMPITO [*presenting* ISMENIA]: By the Twa Gudes, this is the Boeotian Ambassadress that's come tae ye.

LYSISTRATA [*inspecting* ISMENIA]: I should have known – look what a fertile vale she's got there!

CALONICE: Yes, and with all the grass so beautifully cropped, too!

LYSISTRATA: And this one?

LAMPITO: Och, she's a braw bonny lass – a Corinthian.

CALONICE: Yes, I can see why you call her that! [*indicating a prominent part of the Corinthian's person*].

LAMPITO: Who's the convener of this female assembly?

LYSISTRATA: I am.

LAMPITO: Then tell us the noo what ye have tae say.

MYRRHINE: Yes, dear, tell us what this important business is.

LYSISTRATA: I will tell you. But before I do, I want to ask you just one little question.

MYRRHINE: By all means.

LYSISTRATA: The fathers of your children – don't you miss them when they're away at the war? I know not one of you has a husband at home.

CALONICE: I know, my dear. My husband has been away for five months, five months, my dear, in Thrace I think, keeping an eye on our general there.

MYRRHINE: And mine has been in Pylos for the last seven months. –

LAMPITO: And as for my mon, if he ever turns up at home, it's anely to pit a new strap on his shield and fly off again.

LYSISTRATA: That's what it's like. There isn't anyone even to have an affair with – not a sausage! Talking of which, now the Milesians have rebelled, we can't even get our six-inch Ladies' Comforters which we used to keep as leather rations for when all else failed. Well then, if I found a way to do it, would you be prepared to join with me in stopping the war?

MYRRHINE: By the Holy Twain, I would! Even if I had to take off my cloak this very day and – drink!

CALONICE: And so would I – even if I had to cut myself in two, like a flatfish, and give half of myself for the cause.

LAMPITO: And I too, if I had tae climb tae the top o' Taygetus, so I cuid see the licht o' peace whenas I got there.

LYSISTRATA: Then I will tell you my plan: there is no need to keep it back. Ladies, if we want to force our husbands to make peace, we must give up – [*she hesitates.*]

CALONICE: What must we give up? Go on.

LYSISTRATA: Then you'll do it?

CALONICE: If need be, we'll lay down our lives for it.

LYSISTRATA: Very well then. We must give up – sex.

[*Strong murmurs of disapproval, shaking of heads, etc. Several of the company begin to walk off.*]

Why are you turning away from me? Where are you going? What's all this pursing of lips and shaking of heads mean? You're all going pale – I can see tears! Will you do it or won't you? Answer!

MYRRHINE: I won't do it. Better to let the war go on.

CALONICE: I won't do it either. Let the war go on.

LYSISTRATA: Weren't you the flatfish who was ready to cut herself in half a moment ago?

CALONICE: I still am! I'll do that, or walk through the fire, or anything – but give up sex, never! Lysistrata, darling, there's just nothing like it.

LYSISTRATA [*to* MYRRHINE]: How about you?

MYRRHINE: I'd rather walk through the fire too!

LYSISTRATA: I didn't know we women were so beyond redemption. The tragic poets are right about us after all: all we're interested in is having our fun and then getting rid of the baby. My Spartan friend, will you join me? Even if it's just the two of us, we might yet succeed.

LAMPITO: Well – it's a sair thing, the dear knows, for a woman tae sleep alone wi'oot a prick – but we maun do it, for the sake of peace.

LYSISTRATA [*enthusiastically embracing her*]: Lampito, darling, you're the only real woman among the lot of them.

CALONICE: But look, suppose we did give up – what you said – which may heaven forbid – but if we did, how would that help to end the war?

LYSISTRATA: How? Well, just imagine: we're at home, beautifully made up, wearing our sheerest lawn negligées and nothing underneath, and with our – our triangles carefully plucked; and the men are all like ramrods and can't wait to leap into bed, and then we absolutely refuse – that'll make them make peace soon enough, you'll see.

LAMPITO: Din ye mind how Menelaus threw away his sword when he saw but a glimpse of Helen's breasties?

CALONICE: But look, what if they divorce us?

LYSISTRATA: Well, that wouldn't help them much, would it? Like Pherecrates says, it would be no more use than skinning the same dog twice.

CALONICE [*misunderstanding her*]: You know what

you can do with those imitation dogskin things. Anyway, what if they take hold of us and drag us into the bedroom by force?

LYSISTRATA: Cling to the door.

CALONICE: And if they hit us and force us to let go?

LYSISTRATA: Why, in that case you've got to be as damned unresponsive as possible. There's no pleasure in it if they have to use force and give pain. They'll give up trying soon enough. And no man is ever happy if he can't please his woman.

CALONICE: Well – if you really think it's a good idea – we agree.

LAMPITO: And we'll do the same thing and see if we can persuade oor men tae mak peace and mean it. But I dinna see how ye're ever going to get the Athenian riff-raff tae see sense.

LYSISTRATA: We will, you'll see.

LAMPITO: Not sae lang as their warships have sails and they have that bottomless fund o' money in Athena's temple.

LYSISTRATA: Oh, don't think we haven't seen to that! We're going to occupy the Acropolis. While we take care of the sexual side of things, so to speak, all the older women have been instructed to seize the

Acropolis under pretence of going to make sacrifices.

LAMPITO: A guid notion; it soonds as if it will wark.

LYSISTRATA: Well then, Lampito, why don't we confirm the whole thing now by taking an oath?

LAMPITO: Tell us the aith and we'll sweir.

LYSISTRATA: Well spoken. Officeress!

[Enter a SCYTHIAN POLICEWOMAN, *with bow and arrows and a shield. She stares open-eyed about her.*]

Stop gawping like an idiot! Put your shield face down in front of you – so. Now someone give me the limbs of the sacrifical victim.

[*The severed limbs of a ram are handed to her.*]

CALONICE [*interrupting*]: Lysistrata, what sort of oath is this you're giving us?

LYSISTRATA: Why, the one that Aeschylus talks about somewhere, 'filling a shield with blood of fleecy sheep'.

CALONICE: But, Lysistrata, this oath is about peace! We can't possibly take it over a shield.

LYSISTRATA: What do you suggest, then?

CALONICE: Well, if we could slaughter a full-grown cock . . .

LYSISTRATA: You've got a one-track mind.

CALONICE: Well, how *are* you going to take the oath, then?

MYRRHINE: I've got an idea, if you like. Put a large black cup on the ground, and pour some Thasian vine's blood into it, and then we can swear over the cup that we won't – put any water in.

LAMPITO: Whew, that's the kind of aith I like!

LYSISTRATA: A cup and a wine-jar, somebody!

[*These are brought. Both are of enormous size.*]

CALONICE: My dears, isn't it a whopper? It cheers you up even to touch it!

LYSISTRATA: Put the cup down, and take up the sacrificial jar.

[*The attendant elevates the jar, and* LYSISTRATA *stretches out her hands towards it and prays.*]

O holy Goddess of Persuasion, and thou, O Lady of the Loving Cup, receive with favour this sacrifice from your servants the women of Greece. Amen.

[*The attendant begins to pour the wine into the cup.*]

CALONICE: What lovely red blood! And how well it flows!

LAMPITO: And how sweet it smells forby, by Castor!

MYRRHINE [*pushing to the front*]: Let me take the oath first!

CALONICE: Not unless you draw the first lot, you don't!

LYSISTRATA: Lampito and all of you, take hold of the cup. One of you repeat the oath after me, and everybody else signify assent.

[*All put their hands on the cup.* CALONICE *comes forward; and as she repeats each line of the following oath, all the others bow their heads.*]

LYSISTRATA: I will not allow either boyfriend or husband —

CALONICE: I will not allow either boyfriend or husband—

LYSISTRATA: — to approach me in an erect condition. Go on!

CALONICE: — to approach me in an — erect — condition — help, Lysistrata, my knees are giving way! [*She nearly faints, but recovers herself.*]

LYSISTRATA: And I will live at home without any sexual activity —

CALONICE: And I will live at home without any sexual activity —

LYSISTRATA: — wearing my best make-up and my most seductive dresses —

CALONICE: — wearing my best make-up and my most seductive dresses —

LYSISTRATA: — to inflame my husband's ardour.

CALONICE: — to inflame my husband's ardour.

LYSISTRATA: But I will never willingly yield to his desires.

CALONICE: But I will never willingly yield to his desires.

LYSISTRATA: And should he force me against my will —

CALONICE: And should he force me against my will —

LYSISTRATA: I will be wholly passive and unresponsive.

CALONICE: I will be wholly passive and unresponsive.

LYSISTRATA: I will not raise my legs towards the ceiling.

CALONICE: I will not raise my legs towards the ceiling.

LYSISTRATA: I will not take up the lion-on-a-cheese-grater position.

CALONICE: I will not take up the lion-on-a-cheese-grater position.

LYSISTRATA: As I drink from this cup, so will I abide by this oath.

CALONICE: As I drink from this cup, so will I abide by this oath.

LYSISTRATA: And if I do not abide by it, may the cup prove to be filled with water.

CALONICE: And if I do not abide by it, may the cup prove to be filled with water.

LYSISTRATA [*to the others*]: Do you all join in this oath?

ALL: We do.

[CALONICE *drinks from the cup.*]

LYSISTRATA [*taking the cup*]: I'll dispose of the sacred remains.

MYRRHINE: Not all of them, my friend – let's share them, as friends should.

[LYSISTRATA *drinks part of the remaining wine and, with some reluctance, hands the rest to* MYRRHINE. *As she is drinking it off a shout of triumph is heard backstage.*]

LAMPITO: What was that?

LYSISTRATA: What I said we were going to do. The Citadel of Athena is now in our hands. Well then, Lampito, you'll be wanting to go and see to your side of the business at home; but you'd better leave your friends here [*indicating the other Peloponnesian women*] as hostages with us. We'll go up on to the Acropolis now and join the others – the first thing we must do is bar the doors. [*Exit* LAMPITO.]

CALONICE: Won't the men be coming soon to try to get us out?

LYSISTRATA: They can if they like – it won't bother me. Doesn't matter what they threaten to do – even if they try to set fire to the place – they won't make us open the gates except on our own terms.

CALONICE: No, by Aphrodite, they won't. We must show that it's not for nothing that women are called impossible.

[*All the women retire into the Acropolis, and the gates are closed and barred. Enter the* CHORUS OF MEN, *twelve in number, advanced in years, carrying heavy logs and pitchers – the latter containing, as we shall see, lighted embers.*]

LEADER [*recitative*]:
Keep moving, Draces, even if the weight
Of olive wood is hurting your poor shoulder.

CHORUS:
Incredible! Impossible!
    Our women, if you please!
We've kept and fed within our doors
    A pestilent disease!

They've seized our own Acropolis,
    With bars they've shut the gate!

They hold the statue of the Maid,
  Protectress of our state!

Come on and let us hurry there
  And put these logs around,
Smoke out the whole conspiracy
  From Pallas' sacred ground!

With one accord we vote that all
  Have forfeited their life,
And first in the indictment-roll
  (Who else!) stands Lycon's wife.

LEADER:
  And shall these females hold the sacred spot
  That mighty King Cleomenes could not?

CHORUS:
    The grand old Spartan king,
      He had six hundred men,
    He marched them into the Acropolis
      And he marched them out again.
    And he entered breathing fire,
      But when he left the place
    He hadn't washed for six whole years
      And had hair all over his face.

We slept before the gates;
  We wore our shields asleep;
We all of us laid siege to him
  In units twenty deep.
And the King came out half starved,
  And wore a ragged cloak,
And 'I surrender– let me go!'
  Were all the words he spoke.

Now the enemies of the gods
  And of Euripides
Have seized the Acropolis and think
  They can beat us to our knees.
Well, we swear that they will not,
  And we will take them on,
Or else we never fought and beat
  The Medes at Marathon.

LEADER:
  I doubt if I have any hope
Of hauling these logs up the slope.
  My legs they are wonky,
  I haven't a donkey,
But somehow I'll just have to cope.

And I'd better make sure that I've got
Some fire still left in my pot;
   For it would be so sad
   If I thought that I had
And I found in the end that I'd not.

[*He blows on the embers in the pitcher. A pungent
smoke arises, which hurts his eyes.*]
   Yow!
This smoke is so stinging and hot.
I think a mad dog in disguise
Has jumped up and bitten my eyes!
   With precision more fine
   One might call it a swine,
'Cos just look what it's done to my styes.

But come, let us go to the aid
Of Pallas the Warrior-Maid;
   For now is the time,
   As to glory we climb,
And we must not, must not be afraid.

[*Blows on the embers again.*]
   Yow!
This smoke fairly has me dismayed.

Ah, that's woken the old flame up all right, the gods be praised! Now, suppose we put the logs down here, and put tapers into the pots, lighting them first of all of course, and then go for the door like a battering ram? We'll call on them to let the bars down, and if they refuse, then we'll set fire to all the doors and smoke them out. Let's put this stuff down first.

[*They lay down the logs. The* LEADER *has some difficulty in sorting out his logs and his pitcher.*] Ugh! Can the generals in Samos hear us? Will some of them come and help? Well, at least these things aren't crushing my backbone any longer. [*He puts a taper into his pitcher.*] It's up to you now, pot; let's have the coal burning, and let me be the first to have my taper alight. [*Turning towards the shrine of Victory*] Our Lady of Victory, be with us now, and may we set up a trophy to thee when we have conquered the audacious attempt of the women to occupy thy holy Acropolis.

[*The* CHORUS OF MEN *continue to make preparations. Just now, however, the voices of the* CHORUS OF OLD WOMEN, *also twelve in number, are heard in the distance.*]

STRATYLLIS [*off*]:

    I think I see the smoke and vapour rising.
    The fire has started, ladies; we must hasten.

CHORUS OF WOMEN [*off, approaching*]:

        Come, come and help
    Before our friends are fried.
        Some evil men
    Have lit a fire outside.

        Are we too late?
    It's early in the day,
        But at the spring
    We suffered great delay.

        The jostling slaves,
    The crash as pitchers fall,
        The crush, the noise –
    It's no damn fun at all.

    But now I come with water to the aid
    Of thy beleaguered servants, holy Maid!

[*Hereabouts the* WOMEN *begin to enter, carrying pitchers full of water.*]

Some frail old men
Approach with limping gait,
    And carry logs
Of an enormous weight.

    Dire threats they make,
Our friends they hope to see
    Roasted alive.
O Maid, this must not be!

    No, may they save
All Greece from war insane,
    For that is why
They occupy thy fane.

If seeds of fire around thy hill are laid,
Bear water with thy servants, holy Maid!

[STRATYLLIS, *at the* WOMEN's *head, almost collides with the* MEN, *who were just about to begin their rush at the doors.*]

STRATYLLIS: Hold it! What do you think you're up to, you scoundrels?

[*The* LEADER *tries to protest.*]

If you were honest, or had any respect for the gods, you wouldn't be doing what you're doing now.

LEADER: This is the end! A swarm of women come as reinforcements!

STRATYLLIS: What are you so frightened for? We don't outnumber you, after all. Still, remember you haven't seen the millionth part of us yet!

LEADER [*to his neighbour*]: Are we going to let them go on blethering like this? Shouldn't we be bringing down our logs on their backs rather? [*All the* MEN *put down their pitchers.*]

STRATYLLIS [*to her followers*]: Put down your jars too. We don't want any encumbrances in case it comes to a fight.

LEADER [*raising his fist*]: Someone ought to give them a Bupalus or two on the jaw – that might shut them up for a bit.

STRATYLLIS [*presenting her cheek to him*]: All right; there you are; hit me; I won't shy away. Only, if you do, no dog will ever grab your balls again!

LEADER: If you don't shut up, you old crone, I'll knock the stuffing out of you!

STRATYLLIS: If you so much as touch me with the tip of your finger –

LEADER: All right, suppose I do; what then?

STRATYLLIS: I'll bite your chest and tear out your inside!

LEADER [*with calculated insolence*]: Euripides was right! 'There is no beast so shameless as a woman'!

STRATYLLIS [*with cold determination*]: Rhodippe! Everybody! Take up – *jars*! [*They do so.*]

LEADER: Damn you, what have you brought water for?

STRATYLLIS: Well, how about *you*, you warmed-up corpse? What's that fire for? Your funeral?

LEADER: No – those pals of yours, for their funeral.

STRATYLLIS: And we've got the water here to put your fire out!

LEADER: Put our fire out?

STRATYLLIS: You'll see!

[*She prepares to throw the contents of her pitcher on the wood, but the* LEADER *keeps her off with his lighted taper.*]

LEADER: I'm just making up my mind whether to give *you* a roasting.

STRATYLLIS: You wouldn't happen to have any soap, would you? How would you like a bath?

LEADER: A bath, you toothless wonder?

STRATYLLIS: A bridal bath, if you like.

LEADER: Of all the barefaced —

STRATYLLIS: I'm not a slave, you know.

LEADER: I'll shut your big mouth.

STRATYLLIS: If you try, you'll never sit on a jury again.

LEADER: Come on, let's set fire to her hair!

STRATYLLIS: Over to you, water!

[*The* WOMEN *all empty their pitchers over the* MEN, *who are thus thoroughly drenched.*]

MEN:
      Help, I'm soaking!

WOMEN [*with affected concern*]: Was it hot?

MEN:
      No, it certainly was not!
      What're you doing? Let me go!

WOMEN [*continuing to wet them*]:
      We're watering you to make you grow.

MEN:
      Stop it! Stop! I'm numb with cold!

WOMEN: Well, if I may make so bold,
    [*pointing to the* MEN'S *fires*]
      Warm yourselves before the grate.

MEN:
      Stop it! Help! Help! Magistrate!

[*As if in answer to their call, an elderly* MAGIS-TRATE *of severe appearance enters, attended by four* SCYTHIAN POLICEMEN. *The* WOMEN *put*

down their empty pitchers and await develop-
ments. The MAGISTRATE *has not, in fact, come in*
answer to the MEN's *appeal, and he at first takes*
no notice of their bedraggled appearance. Of the
WOMEN *he takes no notice at all.*]

MAGISTRATE: I hear it's the same old thing again — the
unbridled nature of the female sex coming out. All
their banging of drums in honour of that Sabazius
god, and singing to Adonis on the roofs of houses,
and all that nonsense. I remember once in the Assembly — Demostratus, may he come to no good end,
was saying we ought to send the expedition to Sicily,
and this woman, who was dancing on the roof, she
cried, 'O woe for Adonis!', and then he went on and
said we should include some heavy infantry from
Zacynthus, and the woman on the roof — she'd had
a bit to drink, I fancy — she shouted, 'Mourn for
Adonis, all ye people!' But the damnable scoundrel
from Angeriae just blustered on and on. Anyway
[*rather lamely*] that's the sort of outrage that women
get up to.

LEADER: Wait till you hear what this lot have done.
We have been brutally assaulted, and what is more,
we have been given an unsolicited cold bath out of

29

these pots [*kicking one of them and breaking it*], and all our clothes are wringing wet. Anybody would think we were incontinent!

MAGISTRATE: Disgraceful. Disgraceful. But by Poseidon the Shipbuilder, I'm not surprised. Look at the way we pander to the women's vices – we positively teach them to be wicked. That's why we get this kind of conspiracy. Think of when we go to the shops, for example. We might go to the goldsmith's and say, 'Goldsmith, the necklace you made for my wife – she was dancing last night and the clasp came unstuck. Now I've got to go off to Salamis; so if you've got time, could you go down to my place tonight and put the pin back in the hole for her?' Or perhaps we go into a shoemaker's, a great strapping well-hung young fellow, and we say, 'Shoemaker, the toe-strap on my wife's sandal is hurting her little toe – it's rather tender, you know. Could you go down around lunchtime perhaps and ease the strap off for her, enlarge the opening a little?' And now look what's happened! I, a member of the Committee of Ten, having found a source of supply for timber to make oars, and now requiring money to buy it, come to the Acropolis and find the women have shut the doors in my face! No good standing around. Fetch the crowbars, somebody, and we'll soon put a stop to this nonsense. [*To two of the* POLICEMEN] What are you gawping at, you fool? And you? Dreaming about pubs, eh?

[*Crowbars are brought in.*]

Let's get these bars under the doors and lever them up. I'll help.

[*They begin to move the crowbars into position, when* LYSISTRATA, CALONICE *and* MYR-RHINE *open the gates and come out.*]

LYSISTRATA: No need to use force. I'm coming out of my own free will. What's the use of crowbars? It's intelligence and common sense that we need, not violence.

MAGISTRATE: You disgusting creature! Officer! — take her and tie her hands behind her back.

LYSISTRATA: By Artemis, if he so much as touches me, I'll teach him to know his place!

[*The* POLICEMAN *hesitates.*]

MAGISTRATE: Frightened, eh? Go on, the two of you, up-end her and tie her up!

CALONICE [*interposing herself between* SECOND POLICEMAN *and* LYSISTRATA]: If you so much as lay a finger on her, by Pandrosus, I'll hit you so hard you'll shit all over the place.

MAGISTRATE: Obscene language! Officer! [*To* THIRD POLICEMAN] Tie this one up first, and stop her mouth.

MYRRHINE [*interposing herself between* THIRD POLICEMAN *and* CALONICE]: By the Giver of Light, if you touch her, you'll soon be crying out for a cupping-glass!

MAGISTRATE: What's all this? Officer! [*To* FOURTH POLICEMAN] Get hold of her. I'm going to stop this relay some time.

STRATYLLIS [*intervening in her turn*]: By the Bull Goddess, if you go near her, I'll make you scream! [*Giving an exemplary tug to* FOURTH POLICEMAN'S *hair.*]

MAGISTRATE: Heaven help me, I've no more archers! Well, we mustn't let ourselves be worsted by women. Come on, officers, we'll charge them, all together.

LYSISTRATA: If you do, by the Holy Twain, you'll find out that we've got four whole companies of fighting women in there, fully armed.

MAGISTRATE [*calling her bluff*]: Twist their arms behind them, officers.

[*The* POLICEMEN *approach the four women with intent to do this.*]

LYSISTRATA [*to the women inside*]: Come out, the reserve! Lettuce-seed-pancake-vendors of the Market Square! Innkeepers, bakers and garlic-makers! Come to our help!

[*Four bands of women emerge from the Acropolis.*]

Drag them along! Hit them! Shout rude words in their faces!

[*The* POLICEMEN *are quickly brought to the ground, and punched and kicked as they lie there.*]

All right – withdraw – no plunder will be taken.

[*The women retire into the Acropolis.*]

MAGISTRATE [*his hand to his head*]: My bowmen have been utterly defeated!

LYSISTRATA: Well, what did you expect? Did you think we were slaves? Or that women couldn't have any stomach for a fight?

MAGISTRATE: I must admit I thought they only had one for booze.

LEADER:
Our noble magistrate, why waste you words

On these sub-human creatures? Know you not
How we were given a bath when fully clothed,
And that without the benefit of soap?

STRATYLLIS:

Well, he who uses force without good reason
Should not complain on getting a black eye.
We only want to stay at home content
And hurting no one; but if you provoke us,
You'll find you're stirring up a hornets' nest!

CHORUS OF MEN:

Monsters, enough! Our patience now is gone.
    It's time for you to tell
Why you are barricaded here upon
    Our hallowed citadel.

LEADER [*to* MAGISTRATE]:

Now question her, and test her out, and never own
    she's right:
It's shameful to surrender to a girl without a fight.

MAGISTRATE [*to* LYSISTRATA]: Well, the first
thing I want to know is – what in Zeus' name do you
mean by shutting and barring the gates of our own
Acropolis against us?

LYSISTRATA: We want to keep the money safe and
stop you from waging war.

MAGISTRATE: The war has nothing to do with money —

LYSISTRATA: Hasn't it? Why are Peisander and the other office-seekers always stirring things up? Isn't it so they can take a few more dips in the public purse? Well, as far as we're concerned they can do what they like; only they're not going to lay their hands on the money in there.

MAGISTRATE: Why, what are you going to do?

LYSISTRATA: Do? Why, we'll be in charge of it.

MAGISTRATE: *You* in charge of *our* finances?

LYSISTRATA: Well, what's so strange about that? We've been in charge of all your housekeeping finances for years.

MAGISTRATE: But that's not the same thing.

LYSISTRATA: Why not?

MAGISTRATE: Because the money here is needed for the war!

LYSISTRATA: Ah, but the war itself isn't necessary.

MAGISTRATE: Not necessary! How is the City going to be saved then?

LYSISTRATA: We'll save it for you.

MAGISTRATE: You!!!

LYSISTRATA: Us.

MAGISTRATE: This is intolerable!

LYSISTRATA: It may be, but it's what's going to happen.

MAGISTRATE: But Demeter! – I mean, it's against nature!

LYSISTRATA [*very sweetly*]: We've got to save you, after all, sir.

MAGISTRATE: Even against my will?

LYSISTRATA: That only makes it all the more essential.

MAGISTRATE: Anyway, what business are war and peace of yours?

LYSISTRATA: I'll tell you.

MAGISTRATE [*restraining himself with difficulty*]: You'd better or else.

LYSISTRATA: I will if you'll listen and keep those hands of yours under control.

MAGISTRATE: I can't – I'm too livid.

STRATYLLIS [*interrupting*]: It'll be you that regrets it.

MAGISTRATE: I hope it's you, you superannuated crow! [*To* LYSISTRATA] Say what you have to say.

LYSISTRATA: In the last war we were too modest to object to anything you men did – and in any case you wouldn't let us say a word. But don't think we approved! We knew everything that was going on.

Many times we'd hear at home about some major blunder of yours, and then when you came home we'd be burning inside but we'd have to put on a smile and ask what it was you'd decided to inscribe on the pillar underneath the Peace Treaty. And what did my husband always say? 'Shut up and mind your own business!' And I did.

STRATYLLIS: *I* wouldn't have done!

MAGISTRATE [*ignoring her – to* LYSISTRATA]: He'd have given you one if you hadn't!

LYSISTRATA: Exactly – so I kept quiet. But sure enough, next thing we knew you'd taken an even sillier decision. And if I so much as said, 'Darling, why are you carrying on with this silly policy?' he would glare at me and say, 'Back to your weaving, woman, or you'll have a headache for a month. "Go and attend to your work; let war be the care of the menfolk."'

MAGISTRATE: Quite right too, by Zeus.

LYSISTRATA: Right? That we should not be allowed to make the least little suggestion to you, no matter how much you mismanage the City's affairs? And now, look, every time two people meet in the street, what do they say? 'Isn't there a man in the country?'

and the answer comes, 'Not one.' That's why we women got together and decided we were going to save Greece. What was the point of waiting any longer, we asked ourselves. Well now, we'll make a deal. You listen to us – and we'll talk sense, not like you used to – listen to us and keep quiet, as we've had to do up to now, and we'll clear up the mess you've made.

MAGISTRATE: Insufferable effrontery! I will not stand for it!

LYSISTRATA [*magisterially*]: Silence!

MAGISTRATE: You, confound you, a woman with your face veiled, dare to order me to be silent! Gods, let me die!

LYSISTRATA: Well, if that's what's bothering you –
[*During the ensuing trio the women put a veil on the* MAGISTRATE's *head, and give him a sewing-basket and some uncarded wool.*]

LYSISTRATA:

> With veiling bedeck
> Your head and your neck,
> And then, it may be, you'll be quiet.

MYRRHINE: This basket fill full –
CALONICE: By carding this wool –

LYSISTRATA: Munching beans – they're an
                  excellent diet.

                  So hitch up your gown
                  And really get down
              To the job – you could do with
                  some slimmin'.
                  And keep this refrain
                  Fixed firm in your brain –

ALL: That war is the care of the *women*!

[*During the song and dance of the women the*
MAGISTRATE *has been sitting, a ludicrous figure,*
with not the least idea what to do with the wool.
During the following chorus, fuming, he tears off
the veil, flings away wool and basket, and stands
up.]

STRATYLLIS:
    Come forward, ladies: time to lend a hand
    Of succour to our heroine's brave stand!

CHORUS OF WOMEN:
    I'll dance for ever, never will I tire,
        To aid our champions here.
    For theirs is courage, wisdom, beauty, fire;
        And Athens hold they dear.

STRATYLLIS [*to* LYSISTRATA]:

    Now, child of valiant ancestors of stinging-nettle
      stock,

    To battle! – do not weaken, for the foe is seized with
      shock.

LYSISTRATA: If Aphrodite of Cyprus and her sweet
    son Eros still breathe hot desire into our bosoms and
    our thighs, and if they still, as of old, afflict our men
    with that distressing ailment, club-prick – then I
    prophecy that before long we women will be known
    as the Peacemakers of Greece.

MAGISTRATE: Why, what will you do?

LYSISTRATA: Well, for one thing, there'll be no more
    people clomping round the Market Square in full
    armour, like lunatics.

CALONICE: By Aphrodite, never a truer word!

LYSISTRATA: You see them every day – going round
    the vegetable and pottery stalls armed to the teeth.
    You'd think they were Corybants!

MAGISTRATE: Of course: that's what every true
    Athenian ought to do.

LYSISTRATA: But a man carrying a shield with a
    ferocious Gorgon on it – and buying minnows at the
    fishmonger's! Isn't it ridiculous?

CALONICE: Like that cavalry captain I saw, riding round the market with his lovely long hair, buying a pancake from an old stallholder and stowing it in his helmet! And there was a Thracian too – coming in brandishing his light-infantry equipment for all the world as if he were a king or something. The fruit-eress fainted away with fright, and he annexed everything on her stall!

MAGISTRATE: But the international situation at present is in a hopeless muddle. How do you propose to unravel it?

LYSISTRATA: Oh, it's dead easy.

MAGISTRATE: Would you explain?

LYSISTRATA: Well, take a tangled skein of wool for example. We take it so, put it to the spindle, unwind it this way, now that way [*miming with her fingers*]. That's how we'll unravel this war, if you'll let us. Send ambassadors first to Sparta, this way, then to Thebes, that way –

MAGISTRATE: Are you such idiots as to think that you can solve serious problems with spindles and bits of wool?

LYSISTRATA: As a matter of fact, it might not be so idiotic as you think to run the whole City entirely on the model of the way we deal with wool.

MAGISTRATE: How d'you work that out?

LYSISTRATA: The first thing you do with wool is wash the grease out of it; you can do the same with the City. Then you stretch out the citizen body on a bench and pick out the burrs — that is, the parasites. After that you prise apart the club-members who form themselves into knots and clots to get into power, and when you've separated them, pick them out one by one. Then you're ready for the carding: they can all go into the basket of Civic Goodwill — including the resident aliens and any foreigners who are your friends — yes, and even those who are in debt to the Treasury! Not only that. Athens has many colonies. At the moment these are lying around all over the place, like stray bits and pieces of the fleece. You should pick them up and bring them here, put them all together, and then out of all this make an enormous great ball of wool — and from that you can make the People a coat.

MAGISTRATE: Burrs — balls of wool — nonsense! What right have you to talk about these things? What have you done for the war effort?

LYSISTRATA: Done, you puffed-up old idiot! We've contributed to it twice over and more. For one thing, we've given you sons, and then had to send them off to fight.

MAGISTRATE: Enough, don't let's rub the wound.

LYSISTRATA: For another, we're in the prime of our lives, and how can we enjoy it? Even if we've got husbands, we're war widows just the same. And never mind us – think of the unmarried ones, getting on in years and with never a hope – that's what really pains me.

MAGISTRATE: But for heaven's sake, it's not only women that get older.

LYSISTRATA: Yes, I know, but it's not the same thing, is it? A man comes home – he may be old and grey – but he can get himself a young wife in no time. But a woman's not in bloom for long, and if she doesn't succeed quickly, there's no one will marry her, and before long she's going round to the fortune-tellers to ask them if she's any chance.

MAGISTRATE: That's right – any man who's still got a serviceable –

[*Whatever he was going to say, it is drowned by music. During the following trio the women supply him with two half-obols, a filleted head-dress and a wreath, and dress him up as a corpse.*]

LYSISTRATA:
>Shut up! It's high time that you died.
>You'll find a fine coffin outside.
>>Myself I will bake
>>Your Cerberus-cake,
>And here is the fare for the ride.

CALONICE: Look, here are your fillets all red —

MYRRHINE: And here is the wreath for your head —

LYSISTRATA: So why do you wait?
>>You'll make Charon late!
>Push off! Don't you realize? You're
>dead!

MAGISTRATE [*spluttering with rage*]: This is outrageous! I shall go at once and show my colleagues what these women have done to me.

LYSISTRATA: What's your complaint? You haven't been properly laid out? Don't worry; we'll be with you early the day after tomorrow to complete the funeral!

[*The* MAGISTRATE *goes out.* LYSISTRATA, CALONICE *and* MYRRHINE *go back into the Acropolis.*]

LEADER:
>No time to laze; our freedom's now at risk;
>Take off your coats, and let the dance be brisk!

CHORUS OF MEN:

 There's more in this than meets the eye,
  Or so it seems to me.
 The scum will surface by and by:
  It stinks of Tyranny!

 Those Spartan rogues are at their games
  (Their agent's Cleisthenes) —
 It's them that's stirring up these dames
  To seize our jury fees!

LEADER:

 Disgraceful! — women venturing to prate
 In public so about affairs of State!
 They even (men could not be so naïve)
 The blandishments of Sparta's wolves believe!
 The truth the veriest child could surely see:
 This is a Monarchist Conspiracy.
 I'll fight autocracy until the end:
 My freedom I'll unswervingly defend.
 As once our Liberators did, so now
 'I'll bear my sword within a myrtle bough',
 And stand beside them, thus.
 [*He places himself beside the statue of Harmodius and Aristogeiton, imitating the attitude of the latter.*]

                                    And from this place
     I'll give this female one upon the face!
     [*He slaps* STRATYLLIS *hard on the cheek.*]
STRATYLLIS [*giving him a blow in return that sends
     him reeling*]:
     Don't trifle with us, rascals, or we'll show you
     Such fisticuffs, your mothers will not know you!
CHORUS OF WOMEN:
        My debt of love today
        To the City I will pay,
     And I'll pay it in the form of good advice;
        For the City gave me honour
        (Pallas' blessing be upon her!),
     And the things I've had from her deserve their
        price.

        For at seven years or less
        I became a girl priestess
     In the Erechthean temple of the Maid;
        And at ten upon this hill
        I made flour in the mill
     For the cakes which to our Lady are displayed,

        Then I went to Brauron town
        And put on a yellow gown

To walk in the procession as the Bear;
To complete my perfect score
I the sacred basket bore
At Athena's feast when I was young and fair.

STRATYLLIS:

See why I think I have a debt to pay?
'But women can't talk politics,' you say.
Why not? What is it you insinuate?
That we contribute nothing to the State?
Why, we give more than you! See if I lie:
We cause men to be born, you make them die.
What's more, you've squandered all the gains of old,
The Persians' legacy, the allies' gold;
And now, the taxes you yourselves assess
You do not pay. *Who*'s got us in this mess?
Do you complain? Another grunt from you,
And you will feel the impact of this shoe!

[*She takes off her shoes and hits the* MEN'S
LEADER *with it.*]

MEN:

Assault! Assault! This impudence
Gets yet more aggravated.
Why don't we act in self-defence?
Or are we all castrated?

LEADER:

Let's not be all wrapped up, let's show we're men,
Not sandwiches! Take off your cloaks again!

CHORUS OF MEN:

Come, party-sandalled men of war,
The tyrants' foes in days of yore,
    Those days when we were men;
The time has come to grow new wings
And think once more of martial things;
    We must be young again.

LEADER:

If once we let these women get the semblance of a
    start,
Before we know, they'll be adept at every manly
    art.
They'll build a navy, quickly master strategy
    marine,
And fight against the City's fleet, just like that
    Carian queen.
And if to form a cavalry contingent they decide,
They'd soon be teaching *our* equestrian gentry how
    to ride!
For riding on cock-horses suits a woman best of all;
Her seat is sure, and when it bolts she doesn't often fall.

48

Just look at Micon's painting, and you'll see the sort
    of thing:
The Amazonian cavalry engaging Athens' king.
I think that we should seize them now, that's what we
    ought to do,
And shove them in the stocks — and I will start by
    seizing *you*!
    [*He grabs* STRATYLLIS *by the scruff of the neck
    but is forced to let her go by a well-aimed bite.*]

WOMEN:
      Our anger now is all afire,
        And, by the Holy Twain,
      We'll give you such a dose of ire
        You'll scream and scream again.

STRATYLLIS:
  Take off your coats and feel the heart beneath:
  We're women, and our wrath is in our teeth!

CHORUS OF WOMEN:
      The man who lays a hand on me
      Will never more eat celery
        Or beans — he won't be able.
      I burn with anger: I will strike
      And smash his bloody eggs, just like
        The beetle in the fable.

STRATYLLIS:

Friend Lampito from Sparta and Ismenia from the
   north
Are still alive, and so I scorn the threats you vomit
   forth.
You cannot hurt us, though you pass your motions
   six times o'er:
[*pointing at a well-known politician in the audience*]
You're hated by the People here and by the folks
   next door.
The other day I asked a friend to share a sacred meal
To Hecate; my friend (she is a rich Boeotian eel)
Sent word to say, 'I cannot come, my dear; forgive
   me, please;
I can't get through to Athens 'cause of You Know
   Who's decrees.'
These damn decrees will never stop, until we make
   a frontal
Assault on you and grab your legs and make you
   horizontal!
   [*Each of the women grabs a man by the leg and
   brings him to the ground. The* MEN, *defeated,
   retire down stage; the* WOMEN *move closer to the
   Acropolis gates.*]

Act Two

SCENE ONE: *The same. It is five days later.*

[LYSISTRATA *comes out of the Acropolis, in great agitation.*]

STRATYLLIS [*in tragic tones*]:
 Lady who did this daring plot invent,
 Why from thy fortress com'st thou grim-look'd
  out?

LYSISTRATA:
 It is the thoughts of evil women's minds
 That makes me wander restless to and fro.

WOMEN: What sayest thou?

LYSISTRATA: 'Tis true, 'tis true.

STRATYLLIS:
 But what hath caused it? Speak; we are thy friends.

LYSISTRATA:
 Silence is hard, but it were shame to speak.

STRATYLLIS:
 Hide not the ill that we are suffering from.

LYSISTRATA:

I will but one word speak: 'tis sex-starvation.

WOMEN: Alas, great Zeus!

LYSISTRATA: Why cry to Zeus? for 'tis but natural. [*In her ordinary voice*] I just can't keep them to their vow of abstinence any longer. They're deserting. One I caught clearing out the stopped-up hole in the wall near Pan's Grotto — another letting herself down by a rope — another leaving her post as sentry — and there was even one yesterday who was trying to fly down on sparrow-back — aiming straight for the nearest pimpshop! I was able to grab her by the hair and pull her back. And they invent every kind of excuse just to be allowed to go home. Here's one now. [*To* FIRST WOMAN, *who is trying to leave the Acropolis swiftly and stealthily*] Hey, you, where do you think you're going?

FIRST WOMAN: I want to go home. I've got some fleeces there from Miletus, and the moths will be eating them up.

LYSISTRATA: No nonsense about moths! Go back inside.

FIRST WOMAN: But I promise you, I swear, I'll come right back. I'll only spread it out on the bed.

LYSISTRATA: No, you won't; you're not going anywhere.

FIRST WOMAN: Am I to leave my fleeces to be destroyed, then?

LYSISTRATA [*unyielding*]: If necessary, yes.

SECOND WOMAN [*rushing out of the Acropolis*]: Help! My flax, my Amorgian flax! I left it at home without taking the bark off!

LYSISTRATA: Here's another — flax this time. [*To* SECOND WOMAN] Come back.

SECOND WOMAN: But by Artemis I will, as soon as I've stripped it off!

LYSISTRATA: No. Once I let you strip anything off, they'll all be wanting to.

THIRD WOMAN [*coming out as if heavily pregnant*]: Not yet, holy Eilithuia, not yet! Wait till I've got somewhere where it's lawful to give birth!

LYSISTRATA: What's all this nonsense?

THIRD WOMAN: Can't you see? I'm in labour!

LYSISTRATA: But you weren't even pregnant yesterday!

THIRD WOMAN: Well, I am today! Lysistrata, let me go home right away. The midwife's waiting.

LYSISTRATA: What do you think you're talking

about? [*Pokes her stomach.*] Rather hard, isn't it? What have you got there?

THIRD WOMAN: Hard? Yes, of course. It's — it's a baby, a boy.

LYSISTRATA [*tapping it*]: Nonsense! It's made of bronze — and hollow — Let's have a look at it. [*Dives under* THIRD WOMAN'S *dress and emerges with an enormous bronze helmet.*] Athena's sacred helmet! What were you trying to kid me, saying you were pregnant?

THIRD WOMAN: But I am, I swear.

LYSISTRATA: What's this, then?

THIRD WOMAN: Well, I thought — if I found it coming upon me before I got out of the Acropolis — I could nest in the helmet like the pigeons do, and give birth there.

LYSISTRATA: No good trying to get out of it. You're caught. You can stay here until the day your baby [*pointing to the helmet*] is named.

[*Two more women rush out of the Acropolis.*]

FOURTH WOMAN: I can't sleep in there any longer! I've seen the Guardian Serpent!

FIFTH WOMAN: I can't either! Those owls are keeping me awake with their infernal hooting!

LYSISTRATA [*stopping them firmly*]: Tall tales will get you nowhere, ladies. I know you miss your husbands; but don't you realize they miss you as well? Think of the sort of nights they'll be spending! Be strong, sisters; you won't have to endure much longer. There is an oracle [*unrolls a scroll*] that we will triumph if only we don't fall out among ourselves. I have it here. [*The women all gather round.*]

FIFTH WOMAN: What does it say?

LYSISTRATA: Listen. [*Reads.*]

'When that the swallows escape from the hoopoes and gather together,
Keeping away from the cock-birds, then trouble and sorrow will perish,
Zeus will make high into low – '

THIRD WOMAN: What, will we be on top when we do it?

LYSISTRATA:

'But if the swallows rebel and fly from the sacred enclosure,
Then will it manifest be that there is no creature more sex-mad.'

FIFTH WOMAN: Pretty blunt, isn't it? So help us the gods, we won't give up the fight now. Let's go inside.

It would be disgraceful, my dears, wouldn't it, to flag
or fail now we've heard what the oracle says.

[*They all go into the Acropolis. The two* CHO-
RUSES *move to the centre of the stage, facing each
other.*]

MEN:

> I feel a rather pressing need
>   To exercise my tongue:
> I'll tell a little fairy tale
>   I heard when I was young.
>
> Well, once upon a time there was
>   A wise young man who fled
> From women and from marriage, and
>   He roamed the hills instead.
>
> He hunted hares with nets, and had
>   A faithful little hound,
> And hated girls so much he ne'er
>   Came back to his native ground.
>
> Yes, he was truly wise, this lad,
>   Loathed women through and through,
> And following his example we
>   Detest the creatures too.

LEADER [*to* STRATYLLIS]: Give us a kiss.

STRATYLLIS [*slapping him*]: You can take this!

LEADER [*raising his tunic and kicking her*]:

> That's got you there.

STRATYLLIS [*giggling*]:   Look at that hair!

MEN:

> A sign of valour is such hair
>> Upon the crotch, you know;
> Myronides had lots of it,
>> And so had Phormio.

WOMEN:

> I'll tell a little tale myself
>> (I like this little game)
> About a man who had no home,
>> And Timon was his name.
>
> He lived among the thorns and briars,
>> And never served on juries;
> Some said his mother really was
>> A sister of the Furies.
>
> This Timon went away and lived
>> So far from mortal ken
> Not out of hate for women but
>> Because of hate for men.

He loathed them for their wickedness,
    Their company abhorred,
And cursed them loud and long and deep —
But *women* he adored.

STRATYLLIS [*to* LEADER]:
                        One on the cheek! [*Slaps him.*]

LEADER [*in mockery*]:   Oh, how I shriek!

STRATYLLIS: Let's have a go! [*Prepares to kick him.*]

LEADER: Think what you'll show!

[STRATYLLIS *hastily lets her skirt fall again.*]

WOMEN:
    At least, despite our age, it's not
        With hirsute mantle fringed:
    With utmost care and frequently
        Our triangles are singed.

[LYSISTRATA *appears on the battlements. She looks away to the right, and cries out.*]

LYSISTRATA: Women! Women! Come here, quickly!
[*Several women join her, among them* CALONICE *and* MYRRHINE.]

CALONICE: What is it, dear? What are you shouting for?

LYSISTRATA: A man! There's a man coming — and by the look of him he's equipped for the Mysteries of Aphrodite!

CALONICE: Aphrodite, Lady of Cyprus, Paphos and Cythera, as thou hast gone with us till now, so aid us still! — Where is he, whoever he is?

LYSISTRATA: There, down by the shrine of Chloe.

CALONICE: So he is; but who on earth is he?

LYSISTRATA: Have a look, all of you. Does anyone know him?

MYRRHINE: Yes, by Zeus! It's Cinesias, my husband!

LYSISTRATA: Well, dear, you know what you have to do: keep him on toast. Tantalize him. Lead him on. say no, say yes. You can do anything — except what you swore over the cup not to do.

MYRRHINE: Don't worry, I'll do as you say.

LYSISTRATA: I'll stay here and start the process of toasting. Off you go.

[*All go within except* LYSISTRATA.]

[*Enter, right,* CINESIAS *and a* SLAVE, *the latter carrying a* BABY.]

CINESIAS: Gods help me, I'm so bloody stretched out I might just as well be on the rack!

LYSISTRATA: Who goes there?

CINESIAS: Me.

LYSISTRATA: A man?

CINESIAS: I certainly am!

LYSISTRATA: Well, off with you.

CINESIAS: Who do you think you are, sending me away?

LYSISTRATA: I'm on guard duty.

CINESIAS: Well – for the gods' sake – ask Myrrhine to come out to me.

LYSISTRATA: You want me to get you Myrrhine? Who might you be?

CINESIAS: Her husband – Cinesias from Paeonidae.

LYSISTRATA: Cinesias! That name we know well. It's for ever in your wife's mouth. She can't eat an egg or an apple but she says, 'Here's to my love Cinesias.'

CINESIAS [*breathing more rapidly*]: Gods!

LYSISTRATA: It's true, I swear by Aphrodite. And if we happen to get talking about our husbands, she always says, 'The rest are nothing to my Cinesias!'

CINESIAS: Bring her to me! Bring her to me!

LYSISTRATA: Well, aren't you going to give me anything?

CINESIAS: If you want. Look, this is all I've got; catch. [*Throws up a purse of silver.*]

LYSISTRATA: Thanks. I'll go and get her. [*She disappears.*]

CINESIAS: Quickly, please! I've no joy in life any longer since she left home. It pains me to enter the place, it all seems so empty — and my food doesn't agree with me. I'm permanently rigid!

MYRRHINE [*appearing on the battlements, pretending to talk to somebody within*]: I love him, I love him! But he won't love me. Don't ask me to go out to him.

CINESIAS: Myrrie, darling, why on earth not? Come down here.

MYRRHINE: No, I won't.

CINESIAS: Aren't you going to come down when I call you, Myrrhine?

MYRRHINE: You don't really want me.

CINESIAS: What! I'm dying for love of you.

MYRRHINE: I'm going. [*Turns to go back inside.*]

CINESIAS: No — don't — listen to your child!

[*The* SLAVE *caresses the* BABY *without result.*]
Come on, damn you — say 'Mama'! [*Strikes the* BABY.]

BABY: Mama, mama, mama!

CINESIAS: What's wrong with you? Surely you can't harden your heart against your baby! It's five days now since he had a bath or a feed.

MYRRHINE: I pity him all right. His father hasn't looked after him very well.

CINESIAS: For heaven's sake, won't you come down to your own child?

MYRRHINE: How powerful motherhood is! My feelings compel me. I will come down. [*She leaves the battlements.*]

CINESIAS: I think she looks much younger and more beautiful than she was! And all this spurning and coquetting – why, it just inflames my desire even more!

MYRRHINE [*coming out and taking the* BABY *in her arms*]: Come on there, darling, you've got a bad daddy, haven't you? Come on, do you want a little drink, then? [*She feeds him.*]

CINESIAS: Tell me, darling, why do you behave like this and shut yourself up in there with the other women? Why do you give me pain – and yourself too? [*Attempts to caress her breast.*]

MYRRHINE: Keep your hands off me!

CINESIAS: And our things at home – they belong to you as well as me – they're going to ruin!

MYRRHINE [*playing with the* BABY]: I don't care!

CINESIAS: What, you don't care if the chickens are pulling all your wool to pieces?

MYRRHINE: No, I don't.

CINESIAS: And what about the rites of Aphrodite? How long is it since you performed them? [*Puts his arm around her.*] Come along home.

MYRRHINE [*wriggling free*]: No, I won't. Not until you stop the war and make peace.

CINESIAS: Then, if you want, we'll do that.

MYRRHINE: *Then*, if you want, I'll go home. Till then, I've sworn not to.

CINESIAS: But won't you let me make love to you? It's been such a long time!

MYRRHINE: No. Mind you, I'm not saying I don't love you . . .

CINESIAS: You do, Myrrie love? Why won't you let me, then?

MYRRHINE: What, you idiot, in front of the baby?

CINESIAS: No – er – Manes, take it home.

[*The* SLAVE *departs with the* BABY.]

All right, darling, it's out of the way. Let's get on with it.

MYRRHINE: Don't be silly, there's nowhere we can do it here.

CINESIAS: What's wrong with Pan's Grotto?

MYRRHINE: And how am I supposed to purify myself before going back into the Acropolis? It's sacred ground, you know.

CINESIAS: Why, there's a perfectly good spring next to it.

MYRRHINE: You're not asking me to break my oath!

CINESIAS: On my own head be it. Don't worry about that, darling.

MYRRHINE: All right, I'll go and get a camp bed.

CINESIAS: Why not on the ground?

MYRRHINE: By Apollo – I love you very much – but not on the ground! [*She goes into the Acropolis.*]

CINESIAS: Well, at least she does love me, that I can be sure of.

MYRRHINE [*returning with a bare camp bed*]: Here you are. You just lie down, while I take off my – Blast it! We need a – what do you call it? A mattress.

CINESIAS: Mattress? I certainly don't!

MYRRHINE: In the name of Artemis, you're not proposing we should do it on the cords!

CINESIAS: At least give us a kiss first.

MYRRHINE [*doing so*]: There. [*She goes.*]

CINESIAS: Mmmm! Come back quickly!

MYRRHINE [*returning with a mattress*]: There. Now just lie down, and I'll – but look, you haven't got a pillow!

CINESIAS: I don't want one. [*He lies down on the mattress.*]

MYRRHINE: But I do! [*She goes in.*]

CINESIAS: This is a Heracles' supper and no mistake!

MYRRHINE [*returning with a pillow*]: Lift up your head. So.

CINESIAS: That's everything.

MYRRHINE: Everything?

CINESIAS: Yes. Come to me now, precious.

MYRRHINE [*her back to him*]: I'm just undoing my bra. Remember, don't let me down on what you said about making peace.

CINESIAS: May Zeus strike me dead if I do!

MYRRHINE: But look now, you haven't got a blanket!

CINESIAS: But I don't want one! All I want is you, darling!

MYRRHINE: In a moment, love. I'll just pop in for the blanket. [*Goes into the Acropolis.*]

CINESIAS: These bedclothes will be the end of me!

MYRRHINE [*returning with a blanket and a box of ointment*]: Lift yourself up.

CINESIAS: You can see very well I did that long ago.

MYRRHINE: Do you want me to anoint you?

CINESIAS: No, dammit, I don't!

MYRRHINE: Too bad, then, because I'm going to anyway.

CINESIAS [*aside*]: Zeus, make her spill the stuff!

MYRRHINE: Hold out your hand and you can rub it on.

CINESIAS [*smelling the ointment*]: I don't care for it. I only like sexy ones, and besides, this positively reeks of prevarication!

MYRRHINE [*pretending to sniff it in her turn*]: Why, silly me, I brought the wrong one!

CINESIAS: Well, never mind, darling, let it be.

MYRRHINE: Don't talk such nonsense. [*She goes in with the box.*]

CINESIAS: Curse whoever invented these ointments!

MYRRHINE [*returning with another unguent in a bottle*]: Here you are, take this bottle.

CINESIAS: I've got one already and it's fit to burst! [*Indicating what he is referring to.*] Come here and lie down, damn you, and stop this stupid game.

MYRRHINE: I will, I swear it by Artemis. I've got both my shoes off now. But, darling, don't forget about making peace.

CINESIAS: I'll –

> [MYRRHINE *runs off into the Acropolis and the gates slam behind her.*]

She's gone! She's been having me on! Just when I was all ripe for her, she ran away! [*Bursts into sorrowful song.*]

Oh what, tell me what, can this woeful laddie do?
And who, tell me who, can this woeful laddie screw?
Philostratus, I need you, do come and help me quick:
Could I please hire a nurse for my poor young orphan prick?

CHORUS OF MEN:

It's clear, my poor lad, that you're in a baddish way.
And I pity you – O alack and well-a-day!
What heart, what soul, what bollocks could long endure this plight,
Having no one to screw in the middle of the night?

CINESIAS:

O Zeus! Hear me, Zeus! I am suffering tortures dire.

MEN:

    It's that female's fault; she inflamed you with false
      fire.

    I think she is a villain and deserves to suffer death!

WOMEN:

    She's a heroine, and I will praise her while I've breath.

MEN:

    A heroine you call her – to that I'll ne'er agree.
    I'll tell you just what I would really like to see:
    To see a whirlwind catch her, just like a heap of
      hay,
    And to waft her aloft, take her up, up and away.

    Then let the whirlwind drop, after tossing her around
    Till giddy and dizzy she falls back to the ground,
    Where suddenly she finds that there still is more in
      store:
    We'd be queuing and screwing a dozen times or more.

SCENE TWO: *The same.*

[*Enter severally a* HERALD *from Sparta and the
Athenian* MAGISTRATE *we met before. Both appear to*

be suffering from acute priapism but the HERALD *is ineffectually endeavouring to conceal the fact.*]

HERALD: Where are the lairds o' the Athenian council, or the Executive Committee? I wuid hae words wi' them.

MAGISTRATE [*guffawing*]: Ha! ha! ha! What are you – a man or a phallic symbol?

HERALD: My dear lad, I'm a herald, and I'm come frae Sparta tae talk aboot peace.

MAGISTRATE [*pointing*]: Which is why you've got a spear under your clothes, I suppose?

HERALD [*turning his back on him*]: No, I hanna.

MAGISTRATE: What have you turned round for, then? Why are you holding your cloak in that funny way? Did you get a rupture on the way here?

HERALD [*to himself*]: By Castor, the man's senile!

MAGISTRATE: Why, you rascal, you've got prickitis!

HERALD: No, I hanna. Dinna be stupid.

MAGISTRATE: Well, what's that, then?

HERALD: It's a standard Spartan cipher rod.

MAGISTRATE [*indicating his counterpart*]: Yes, and so is this. You needn't think I'm a fool; you can tell me the truth. What is the present situation in Sparta?

HERALD: Tae be colloquial, things ha' reached a total

cock-up. All our allies ha' risen, and we canna get hold o' Pellene. [*Looks longingly at the* WOMEN'S CHORUS.]

MAGISTRATE: What's the cause of it all? Do you think Pan was responsible?

HERALD: Pan? Och, no, it was Lampito, and then a' the ither women – almost as though there were some kind of plot in it – they a' pit up a Keep Oot notice over their whatnots.

MAGISTRATE: So how are you getting on?

HERALD: Verra badly, verra badly. We a' bend double as we walk roond the toon, as though we were carrying lamps. D'ye ken, the women won't even let us sae much as touch their knobs, till we a' consent tae mak a general peace for the whole of Greece.

MAGISTRATE: Ah, now I see the plot! They're all in it – all the women everywhere. Tell your people at once to send delegates here with full powers to negotiate for peace. I'll go and tell the Council to choose delegates to represent Athens. When they see my – my cipher rod I don't think they'll hesitate a moment.

HERALD: That's a' fine by me. I'll fly.

[*Exeunt severally.*]

[*The two* CHORUSES *advance.*]

LEADER:

There is no beast more stubborn than a woman,
And neither fire nor leopard is more shameless.

STRATYLLIS:

If you know that, why do you hate us so?
We would be faithful friends, if you would let us.

LEADER:

Women I loathe, both now and evermore.

STRATYLLIS:

Well, as you please. But really, you look stupid
Without your coat. Come on now, put it on.
Or no, I know, I'll put your coat on for you.

LEADER [*when she has done so*]:

That was a good turn that you did to me,
And I was wrong to yield to wrath and doff it.

STRATYLLIS:

There, you look better now, and not so comic.
And now, if you'll keep still, I'll take that gnat
Out of your eye.

LEADER:

              A gnat! that's what it was
Was biting me! Come, dig it out and show me.
I've had these bites for hours and hours and
hours.

STRATYLLIS:

    All right. [*She explores his eye carefully; he*
       winces.]

             You *are* a difficult old man.
    Great Zeus, it's monstrous! Look, just look at it!
    It must be from the Marsh of Marathon!

LEADER:

    Thank you so much. The gnat was digging deep,
    And now the tears are streaming from my eyes.

STRATYLLIS:

    Don't worry, I've a handkerchief to wipe them –
    You *are* a bad old man, you know – and now
    I'll kiss you.

LEADER:

           No, you don't.

ALL THE WOMEN: Oh, yes, we do!

    [*And each of them kisses one of the* MEN.]

LEADER:

    Damn you, you wheedlers! Still the saying's true –
    We can't live with you, we can't live without you!
    Let us make peace, that's what we ought to do;
    You won't hit us, we promise not to flout you;
      Let us all form a single happy ring
      And in that union our next number sing.

[*The two* CHORUSES *join hands and are from now on united in a single chorus. They sing the following two songs together.*]

No citizen need fear that we
   Will dent his reputation;
We rather think you've had enough
   Of toil and tribulation.

So what we'll do is not to jest
   Or try to be buffoons;
Instead we'd like to publicize
   Some unexpected boons.

If anyone is short of drachs,
   Two hundred (say) and twenty,
Just call on us, because we've got
   Good money-bags in plenty,

It's true they have no cash inside;
   Still, I should not complain:
That means that you will never need
   To pay it back again!

I'm entertaining some friends from Carystus
   tonight, tonight,
The table's prepared and you'll find the menu just
   right, just right.

There's plenty of soup and I've sacrificed a sow, a
   sow,
And – I think I can smell it – the pork should be
   roasting now, 'sting now.

You'd best be quick; it's a well-attended affair, affair,
So bath the kids and then get along right there,
   right there.
Walk in – no questions – pretend that you're in
   your own place, own place;
There's just one thing: the door will be shut in your
   face, your face.
   [*Enter a group of* SPARTAN AMBASSADORS,
   again looking very distended.]

LEADER:
   Here come our bearded Spartan friends. Why,
      anyone would swear
   That each of them was carrying a pig-pen under
      there!
   Welcome, gentlemen. How are you?
AMBASSADOR: I dinna need tae answer that in words;
   ye can see for yersel's how we are.
LEADER: Whew! You're certainly under severe tension
   – I should say things were quite inflammatory.

74

AMBASSADOR: And that's no lie. We dinna mind where, we dinna mind how, but we maun hae peace!

[*Enter several* ATHENIAN NEGOTIATORS.]

LEADER: Ah, here are our true-born Athenian representatives. Look as if they'd dropped from a great height and broken their backs, the way they're bending over. Yes, definitely a case of dropsy, I'd say. And look how they're holding their clothes miles away from their bodies!

NEGOTIATOR: Will somebody tell us where Lysistrata is? We're at the *point* of collapse.

LEADER: You've both got the same thing, I think. When does it get you worst? In the small hours?

NEGOTIATOR: Not just then – all the time – and it's killing us. If we don't make peace right away, we shall all end up screwing Cleisthenes.

[*The* SPARTAN AMBASSADORS *take off their coats.*]

LEADER: I shouldn't do that if I were you. You wouldn't want your sacred emblems mutilated, would you?

NEGOTIATOR [*to* AMBASSADOR]: They're right, you know.

AMBASSADOR: I'm thinking so too. Here, let's pit them on again.

NEGOTIATOR: Well now, old chap, this is a pretty pass we've all come to!

AMBASSADOR: Not sae bad as it wuid be, my dear fellow, if one of those amateur sculptors saw us like this.

NEGOTIATOR: Anyway, to business. What are you here for?

AMBASSADOR: Tae mak peace.

NEGOTIATOR: That's good to hear. So are we. Why don't we ask Lysistrata to come out? She's the only one who can reconcile us properly.

AMBASSADOR: Ay, by the Twa Gudes, Lysistratus, Lysistrata, Lysistratum, masculine, feminine or neuter, I couldna care less, sae we can bring this war to an end!

[*Music. The Propylaea opens wide, and* LYSIS-TRATA *appears, magnificently arrayed.*]

NEGOTIATOR: No need to summon her, it seems; here she is!

CHORUS:
Mighty lady with a mission –
   O Paragon of common sense –
Running fount of erudition –
   Miracle of eloquence!

Greece is torn, and would be healed;
War is rife – let peace be sealed;
Thou hast conquered by thy charm;
Make the cities all disarm.
Mighty lady with a mission –
Paragon of common sense –
Running fount of erudition –
Miracle of eloquence!

LYSISTRATA: It's not hard, if you catch them when they're aroused but not satisfied. We'll soon see. Reconciliation!

[*An extremely beautiful and totally unclothed girl enters from the Acropolis.*]

Bring the Spartans to me first of all. Don't be rough or brusque; handle them very gently, not in the brutal way men lay hold on us, but the way a lady should – very civilized.

[RECONCILIATION *goes up to one of the* SPARTAN AMBASSADORS *and offers him her hand. He refuses.*]

Well, if he won't give you his hand, try that leather thing. That's right. Now the Athenians. You can take hold of anything they offer you. Now you, Spartans, stand on this side of me, and you, Athenians, on the other side, and listen to what I have to say.

[*The* AMBASSADORS *and* NEGOTIATORS, *guided by* RECONCILIATION, *take their places on either side of* LYSISTRATA.]

I am a woman, but I am not brainless:
I have my share of native wit, and more,
Both from my father and from other elders
Instruction I've received. Now listen, both:
Hard will my words be, but not undeserved.
You worship the same gods at the same shrines,
Use the same lustral water, just as if
You were a single family — which you are —
Delphi, Olympia, Thermopylae —
How many other Panhellenic shrines
Could I make mention of, if it were needed!
And yet, although the Mede is at our gates,
You ruin Greece with mad intestine wars.
This is my first reproach to both of you.

NEGOTIATOR [*who has been eyeing* RECONCILI-ATION *all through this speech*]: I hope she doesn't take much longer. I doubt if this giant carrot will stand it.

LYSISTRATA:

The next is for the Spartans. Know you not
How Pericleidas came to Athens once,
And sat a suppliant at our holy altar,
In scarlet uniform and death-white face,
Beseeching us to send a force to help you?
For then two perils threatened you at once:
The Helots, and Poseidon with his earthquake.
So Cimon took four thousand infantry
And saved the Spartan people from destruction.
This, Spartans, the Athenians did for you:
Is it then just to ravage Athens' land?

NEGOTIATOR: Yes, Lysistrata, they're in the wrong.

AMBASSADOR: We are. But by the Twa Gudes, she's a
fine bottom.

LYSISTRATA:

Think not, Athenians, you are guiltless either.
Remember once you had to dress like slaves,
Until the Spartans came in force, and slew
The foreign mercenaries of Hippias
And many of his allies and confederates.
They fought for you alone upon that day
And set you free, removed your servile cloak
And clothed you with Democracy again.

AMBASSADOR [*still intent on* RECONCILIATION]: I havena seen a bonnier lass.

NEGOTIATOR: Nor I a shapelier cunt.

LYSISTRATA:
> So why on fighting are your hearts so set?
> For each of you is in the other's debt.

Why don't you make peace? What's the problem?

AMBASSADOR [*who has got hold of* RECONCILIATION; *both he and his opposite number map out their demands on her person*]: We will, if ye'll give us back this little promontory.

NEGOTIATOR: Which one, sir?

AMBASSADOR: Pylos. We've set oor hearts on it and been prod-prodding at it for years.

NEGOTIATOR: By Poseidon, you shan't have it!

LYSISTRATA: Give it them.

NEGOTIATOR: Who will we have left to stimulate, then? To revolt, I mean.

LYSISTRATA: Well, you ask for somewhere else in exchange.

NEGOTIATOR: Very well . . . give us [*mapping the areas out*] first of all the Echinian triangle here, then the Malian Gulf — I mean the one round behind, of course, — and lastly — er — the Long Legs — I mean the Long Walls of Megara.

AMBASSADOR: Are ye crazy? There's naething left!

LYSISTRATA: Come now, don't quarrel over a pair of legs — I mean walls.

NEGOTIATOR: I'm ready to go back to my husbandry now.

AMBASSADOR: And I'm wanting tae do some manuring.

LYSISTRATA: Time enough for that when you've made peace. If that's what you want to do, go and have a conference with your allies and agree it with them.

NEGOTIATOR: Allies, ma'am? — look at the state we're in! We know what the allies will say — the same as we do: 'Peace! Peace! Bed! Bed!'

AMBASSADOR: And oors the same.

NEGOTIATOR: And we certainly needn't ask the Carystians.

LYSISTRATA: Fine then. Now we had better ratify the treaty in the usual way. The women will entertain you in the Acropolis; they have plenty of good food in their picnic baskets. And over that you can clasp

hands and take the oaths. And then, let everyone take
his wife and live happily ever after!

NEGOTIATOR: Let's go right away.

AMBASSADOR: Lead the way, my dear.

NEGOTIATOR: Yes, and quickly.

[*All except the* CHORUS *go inside.*]

CHORUS:

Embroidered upholstery – magnificent cloaks –
    Fine ornaments fashioned of gold:
If your daughter is chosen the Basket to bear,
    Don't ask where these items are sold.

For all that I've got for the taking is yours;
    The seals on the boxes are weak;
Remove them, and then from whatever's inside
    Take just what it is that you seek.

There's one little thing I should warn you of first,
    For if not, I'd be being unfair:
That unless you have got sharper eyesight than me,
    You'll find there ain't anything there!

        If anyone who's short of bread
        Has slaves and kids that must be fed,
        I've got some loaves of finest milling,
        Quadruple size, and very filling.

Let any who provisions lack
Come round to me with bag or sack;
My servant is enjoined by me
To give them all these loaves for free.

One thing I should have said before —
They'd better not come near the door;
I have a dog who at the sight
Of strangers will not bark but bite.

[*Some* LAYABOUTS *come in, and begin pounding on the Acropolis gates.*]

FIRST LAYABOUT: Open up! Open up!

DOORKEEPER [*coming to the door*]: Get away from here!

FIRST LAYABOUT [*to his companions*]: What are you waiting for? [*To the* DOORKEEPER *and others inside*] Do you want me to burn you up with my torch? No, on second thoughts, that's an absolute comic cliché and I won't do it.

[*Protests from the audience.*]

Oh — very well — to please you, I'll go through with it.

SECOND LAYABOUT: And we'll be with you.

DOORKEEPER [*coming out*]: Get off with you! I'll pull your long hair out! Shoo! Get out of the way of the

Spartans – the banquet's nearly over, and they'll soon be coming out!

[*He drives them away and goes back inside. Presently the door opens, and two well-fed* ATHENIAN DINERS *emerge.*]

FIRST DINER: Never known a party like it. The Spartans were the life and soul of it, weren't they? And we were pretty clever, considering how sozzled we were.

SECOND DINER: Not surprising really. We couldn't be as stupid as we are when we're sober. If the Athenians took my advice they'd always get drunk when going on diplomatic missions. As it is, you see, we go to Sparta sober, and so we're always looking for catches. We don't hear what they do say, and we hunt for implications in what they don't say – and we bring back quite incompatible reports of what went on. And yet we only have to have a few, and everything's all right. Even if one of them starts singing 'Telamon' when he should be singing 'Cleitagora', all we do is slap him on the back and swear that 'Telamon' was just what was wanted!

[*They go out. The* LAYABOUTS *return.*]

DOORKEEPER: Here come these no-goods again. Bugger off, all of you!

FIRST LAYABOUT: We'd better. They're coming out.
  [*They run off.*]
  [*Enter* ATHENIANS *and* SPARTANS, *one of whom carries bagpipes.*]
SPARTAN: Here, my dear fellow, tak the pipes, and I'll dance a reel and sing a song in honour of the Athenians and of oursel's forby.
ATHENIAN: Yes, do. There's nothing I enjoy so much as a good old Spartan dance.
  [*The* PIPER *takes the pipes and strikes up. The* SPARTAN *dances a solo as he sings.*]

> Raise the song o' Sparta's fame,
> And tae valiant Athens' name
> Kindle an undying flame,
>   Holy Memory.
>
> How they focht in days of yore
> Off the Artemisium shore —
> They were few, the Medes were more —
>   Theirs the victory!
>
> While we Spartans quit oor hame —
> Boarlike from oor mouths ran faem —
> Brave our King, and high our aim —
>   'Hellas shall be free!'

Nocht cuid frighten us that day,
Nocht cuid mak us run away,
And we won renown for aye
    At Thermopylae.

Artemis the Virgin Queen,
Huntress in the wuids sae green,
Come and bless this happy scene,
    Come, we call on thee!

Pour thy grace upon oor peace;
Make the artful foxes cease;
Let guidwill and love increase
    And prosperity!

[*The Propylaea opens wide, and* LYSISTRATA
*appears, flanked by all the Athenian and Spartan
women.*]

LYSISTRATA: Well, gentlemen, it's all happily settled.
Spartans, here are your wives back. And here are yours.
Now form up everyone, two by two, and let us have a
dance of thanksgiving.

    And may the gods vouchsafe to give us sense
    Ne'er to repeat our former dire offence!

CHORUS:

Come, let us on the Graces call,
Apollo next who healeth all,
On Artemis and Hera too,
On Bacchus and his Maenad crew,
And most on Zeus above:

Let all the gods come witness now
The making of our solemn vow
To stay our hands from mutual war
And keep the peace for evermore
Made by the power of Love.

O great Apollo, hail!
O let it be that we
May win the victory!
O great Apollo, hail!
O great Apollo, hail!
Evoi! Evoi! Evoi!

[*The* CHORUS *dance joyfully out. The* ATHEN-
IANS *and* SPARTANS *and their wives remain.*]

LYSISTRATA [*recitative*]:

To hail the peace for which we've pined so long,
There's a time, I fancy, for another song!

SPARTAN:

[*as a spectacular dance is performed by a soloist and everyone else dances in the background*]

Muse, now be Sparta praisin',
Muse, Phoebus' name be raisin',
And in her temple brazen
   Let Pallas hear:
Come, sons of Tyndareus's,
Castor and Polydeuces,
Favourites of a' the Muses,
   Famed far and near.

Dance, dance tae Sparta's might!
Swing, swing yer sheepskins light!
Let's praise oor noble city,
   Home o' songs and dances pretty –
Home of the sacred chorus,
Home of our sires before us,
Stout shield and mantle o'er us,
   Sparta the brave!

Girls, shake your pretty tresses,
Whirl roond yer Doric dresses,
See your display expresses
   Joy and relief:

Joy at the end o' slaughter –
See, Leda's beauteous daughter,
Purer than mountain water,
   Helen's the chief.

   Dance, dance for Helen fair!
   Smooth, smooth yer flowing hair!
   Tak off wi' both yer feet and
   Stamp on every ither beat and
Pray that Athena never
Her link tae Sparta sever,
May she protect for ever
   Sparta the brave!
[*All kneel facing the shrine of Victory.*]

ALL:

   Athena, hail, thou Zeus-born Maid!
   Who war and death in Greece hast stayed:
   Hail, fount from whom all blessings fall;
   All hail, all hail, Protectress of us all!
[*General dance.*]

APOLLONIUS OF RHODES · *Jason and the Argonauts*
ARISTOPHANES · *Lysistrata*
SAINT AUGUSTINE · *Confessions of a Sinner*
JANE AUSTEN · *The History of England*
HONORÉ DE BALZAC · *The Atheist's Mass*
BASHŌ · *Haiku*
AMBROSE BIERCE · *An Occurrence at Owl Creek Bridge*
JAMES BOSWELL · *Meeting Dr Johnson*
CHARLOTTE BRONTË · *Mina Laury*
CAO XUEQIN · *The Dream of the Red Chamber*
THOMAS CARLYLE · *On Great Men*
BALDESAR CASTIGLIONE · *Etiquette for Renaissance Gentlemen*
CERVANTES · *The Jealous Extremaduran*
KATE CHOPIN · *The Kiss and Other Stories*
JOSEPH CONRAD · *The Secret Sharer*
DANTE · *The First Three Circles of Hell*
CHARLES DARWIN · *The Galapagos Islands*
THOMAS DE QUINCEY · *The Pleasures and Pains of Opium*
DANIEL DEFOE · *A Visitation of the Plague*
BERNAL DÍAZ · *The Betrayal of Montezuma*
FYODOR DOSTOYEVSKY · *The Gentle Spirit*
FREDERICK DOUGLASS · *The Education of Frederick Douglass*
GEORGE ELIOT · *The Lifted Veil*
GUSTAVE FLAUBERT · *A Simple Heart*
BENJAMIN FRANKLIN · *The Means and Manner of Obtaining Virtue*
EDWARD GIBBON · *Reflections on the Fall of Rome*
CHARLOTTE PERKINS GILMAN · *The Yellow Wallpaper*
GOETHE · *Letters from Italy*
HOMER · *The Rage of Achilles*
HOMER · *The Voyages of Odysseus*

PENGUIN 60s CLASSICS

HENRY JAMES · *The Lesson of the Master*
FRANZ KAFKA · *The Judgement* and *In the Penal Colony*
THOMAS À KEMPIS · *Counsels on the Spiritual Life*
HEINRICH VON KLEIST · *The Marquise of O—*
LIVY · *Hannibal's Crossing of the Alps*
NICCOLÒ MACHIAVELLI · *The Art of War*
SIR THOMAS MALORY · *The Death of King Arthur*
GUY DE MAUPASSANT · *Boule de Suif*
FRIEDRICH NIETZSCHE · *Zarathustra's Discourses*
OVID · *Orpheus in the Underworld*
PLATO · *Phaedrus*
EDGAR ALLAN POE · *The Murders in the Rue Morgue*
ARTHUR RIMBAUD · *A Season in Hell*
JEAN-JACQUES ROUSSEAU · *Meditations of a Solitary Walker*
ROBERT LOUIS STEVENSON · *Dr Jekyll and Mr Hyde*
TACITUS · *Nero and the Burning of Rome*
HENRY DAVID THOREAU · *Civil Disobedience* and *Reading*
LEO TOLSTOY · *The Death of Ivan Ilyich*
IVAN TURGENEV · *Three Sketches from a Hunter's Album*
MARK TWAIN · *The Man That Corrupted Hadleyburg*
GIORGIO VASARI · *Lives of Three Renaissance Artists*
EDITH WHARTON · *Souls Belated*
WALT WHITMAN · *Song of Myself*
OSCAR WILDE · *The Portrait of Mr W. H.*

ANONYMOUS WORKS

Beowulf and Grendel
Buddha's Teachings
Gilgamesh and Enkidu
Krishna's Dialogue on the Soul
Tales of Cú Chulaind
Two Viking Romances

READ MORE IN PENGUIN

For complete information about books available from Penguin and how to order them, please write to us at the appropriate address below. Please note that for copyright reasons the selection of books varies from country to country.

IN THE UNITED KINGDOM: Please write to *Dept. EP, Penguin Books Ltd, Bath Road, Harmondsworth, Middlesex UB7 0DA.*

IN THE UNITED STATES: Please write to *Consumer Sales, Penguin USA, P.O. Box 999, Dept. 17109, Bergenfield, New Jersey 07621-0120.* VISA and MasterCard holders call 1-800-253-6476 to order Penguin titles.

IN CANADA: Please write to *Penguin Books Canada Ltd, 10 Alcorn Avenue, Suite 300, Toronto, Ontario M4V 3B2.*

IN AUSTRALIA: Please write to *Penguin Books Australia Ltd, P.O. Box 257, Ringwood, Victoria 3134.*

IN NEW ZEALAND: Please write to *Penguin Books (NZ) Ltd, Private Bag 102902, North Shore Mail Centre, Auckland 10.*

IN INDIA: Please write to *Penguin Books India Pvt Ltd, 706 Eros Apartments, 56 Nehru Place, New Delhi 110 019.*

IN THE NETHERLANDS: Please write to *Penguin Books Netherlands bv, Postbus 3507, NL-1001 AH Amsterdam.*

IN GERMANY: Please write to *Penguin Books Deutschland GmbH, Metzlerstrasse 26, 60594 Frankfurt am Main.*

IN SPAIN: Please write to *Penguin Books S. A., Bravo Murillo 19, 1º B, 28015 Madrid.*

IN ITALY: Please write to *Penguin Italia s.r.l., Via Felice Casati 20, I-20124 Milano.*

IN FRANCE: Please write to *Penguin France S. A., 17 rue Lejeune, F-31000 Toulouse.*

IN JAPAN: Please write to *Penguin Books Japan, Ishikiribashi Building, 2-5-4, Suido, Bunkyo-ku, Tokyo 112.*

IN GREECE: Please write to *Penguin Hellas Ltd, Dimocritou 3, GR-106 71 Athens.*

IN SOUTH AFRICA: Please write to *Longman Penguin Southern Africa (Pty) Ltd, Private Bag X08, Bertsham 2013.*